Praise for

"*Be BIG* should remind every leader of an organization that stepping up, stepping out, and being bold is very difficult for many and impossible for all if the leader doesn't create an environment of 'Be BIG' to Win BIG."

Larry D. DeShon, Executive Vice President
of Operations, Avis Budget Group

"*Be BIG* simply and clearly offers tips you can implement at work tomorrow to help you and your company reach your very best."

Dr. Mark S. Albion, cofounder, Net Impact,
and *New York Times* bestselling author of
Making a Life, Making a Living and *True to
Yourself: Leading a Values-Based Business*

"This book offers me a simple reminder that it is my responsibility as a leader and manager to help those who work for me to be their BIG selves. Seeing myself as BIG and seeing my team as BIG positions us to do our best work together!"

Cindy Szadokierski, Vice President,
Operational Services, United Express and Ted

"*Be BIG* is a deceptively simple presentation of some important ideas about reaching your potential as a person and as a team member. In our increasingly interdependent world, learning how to 'Step Up, Step Out, and Be Bold' in ways that enable others to do the same is a vitally important skill."

L. David Brown, Associate Director for
International Programs, Hauser Center for
Nonprofit Organizations, Harvard University

"*Be BIG* illustrates how throwing off what limits us and our interaction allows us to excel and to enjoy our true potential."

Joel Lamstein, President, John Snow, Inc.
World Education

"*Be BIG* offers profound insights into simple yet powerful ideas to enable people to show up BIG in life and contribute fully in their work."

Maya Hu-Chan, President,
Global Leadership Associates

"Judith and Fred are challenging us to grow up and be present! We live in a time when we need our best selves to confront the increasingly complex economic, social, and technical problems of our society. Their call is both brave and essential. I believe that if you dare to step into this book with both feet, you will come away with more than you ever imagined—for yourself, for others, and for the world."

Sandra Janoff, PhD, Codirector,
Future Search Network

"Everyone who works with or for an organization needs to read this book and practice the messages. *Be BIG* is fun, easy to read, and powerful. I wish I would have had it to read ages ago when I first went to work for a corporation."

Julie O'Mara, President, O'Mara and Associates,
and author of *Diversity Activities and Training Designs*

"The universal answer on how to live has never been told in such a clear, simple, and compelling manner. The practical operating instructions for living a fulfilled life are all here in this short, timeless book."

Claude F. G. Elsen, Managing Partner, Consilux

"Judith and Fred have again given us a gift and extended to us a wonderful invitation to set our mind on a Be BIG channel. This book will engage us to help others and help ourselves move toward a very daring but rewarding challenge . . . taking the time to create the WE."

Mila N. Baker, PhD, Vice President,
Human Resources, SourceMedia Publishing

BE
BIG

Step Up
Step Out
Be Bold

Judith H. Katz
Frederick A. Miller

daring to do our best work together

BK

Berrett–Koehler Publishers, Inc.
San Francisco
a BK Business book

Berrett-Koehler Publishers, Inc.
235 Montgomery Street, Suite 650
San Francisco, CA 94104-2916
Tel: (415) 288-0260   Fax: (415) 362-2512   www.bkconnection.com

Ordering Information
Quantity sales. Special discounts are available on quantity purchases by corporations, associations, and others. For details, contact the "Special Sales Department" at the Berrett-Koehler address above.

Individual sales. Berrett-Koehler publications are available through most bookstores. They can also be ordered directly from Berrett-Koehler: Tel: (800) 929-2929; Fax: (802) 864-7626; www.bkconnection.com.

Orders for college textbook/course adoption use. Please contact Berrett-Koehler: Tel: (800) 929-2929; Fax: (802) 864-7626.

Orders by U.S. trade bookstores and wholesalers. Please contact Ingram Publisher Services: Tel: (800) 509-4887; Fax: (800) 838-1149; E-mail: customer.service@ingrampublisherservices.com; or visit www.ingram publisherservices.com/Ordering for details about electronic ordering.

Berrett-Koehler and the BK logo are registered trademarks of Berrett-Koehler Publishers, Inc.

Printed in the United States of America

Berrett-Koehler books are printed on long-lasting acid-free paper. When it is available, we choose paper that has been manufactured by environmentally responsible processes. These may include using trees grown in sustainable forests, incorporating recycled paper, minimizing chlorine in bleaching, or recycling the energy produced at the paper mill.

Library of Congress Cataloging-in-Publication Data
Katz, Judy H., 1950-
 Be big : step up, step out, be bold : daring to do our best work together / Judith H. Katz and Frederick A. Miller. — 1st ed.
 p. cm.
 ISBN 978-1-57675-452-8 (pbk. : alk. paper)
 1. Interpersonal relations. 2. Interpersonal communication. 3. Organizational behavior. I. Miller, Frederick A., 1946- II. Title.
 HM1166.K38   2008
 302—dc22   2008010832

Illustrations by Jeevan Sivasubramaniam.
Composition by Beverly Butterfield, Girl of the West Productions.

FIRST EDITION
13 12 11   10 9 8 7 6 5

With love to David, my life partner,
who consistently has faith in my Being BIG;
Fred, who has taught me the meaning of being
my best self—and what daring to do our best
work together *really means; and Corey,*
for your unrelenting support of this
project and everything I do.

JHK

With love to Pauline Kamen Miller,
Corey Jamison, Ava Albert Schnidman,
Carol Brantley, Edie Seashore, my mother,
"dad" Katz, Watson L. Williams, Kaleel,
and all the clients who have
encouraged me to Be BIG.

FAM

Contents

||||||||||||||||||||||||||||||||||||||||||||||||||||||||||||||

Introduction

The Need to Be BIG

I am daring you to think bigger,
to act bigger and to be bigger.

I dare you to think creatively.

I dare you to . . . lead and
inspire others.

I dare you to build character.

I dare you to share.

I am promising you a richer life
and more exciting life if you do.

Excerpts from William H. Danforth, *I Dare You!*
(St. Louis, MO: American Youth Foundation, 1931).

William H. Danforth (1870–1956),
founder of the Ralston Purina Company.

Organizations need us to bring more of ourselves to work

Many of us know a secret that is rarely spoken: too many of us in most organizations are hiding things. Important things.

We are hiding *our full selves*!

Sometimes we hide just parts of ourselves. Sometimes we hide all of ourselves.

By not letting our full selves be seen, we make ourselves small.

Yet within many of us is often another secret. An even BIGger secret.

Many of us have a strong desire to Be BIG.

To give our best every day.
To not hide out or be small.

To **Be BIG** is not about ego or fame. It is not about showing off or showing others up.

Many of us want to **Be BIG** in order to bring our voice and add great value— and to enable our coworkers and partners to do the same.

To **Be BIG** is a life stance of learning and growing and partnering with others.

Some are fortunate to be able to live life BIG every day, but many others have not yet found a way to **Be BIG**. They feel they need to stay hidden and be their small selves.

Why?

Why does it feel safer to be small?

While some of us may feel small because we lack self-confidence, certain management styles and workplace cultures contribute as well.

In some organizations, it can be dangerous to **Be BIG** enough to stand out. It can be dangerous to step out of the box you, or others, have put you in.

||||||||||||||||||||||||||||||||||||||||||||||||||||||||||||||

It can get you criticized.

It can get you ostracized.

It can get you fired.

So a lot of us are in stealth mode.
We are trying to fly under the radar.

We are trying to stay out of sight.

We are trying to blend in with the
landscape. We want to appear
harmless, nonthreatening, small.

We are keeping our heads down and
even encouraging others around us
to do the same.

And for many of us, the thought of
being BIG is positively frightening.

||||||||||||||||||||||||||||||||||||||||||||||||||||||||||||||||

Most organizations today are in a competitive struggle for their very survival.

Organizations need all of us to bring more of ourselves to the workplace.

Innovation, problem solving, and productivity depend upon us being BIG. Each person must contribute to collectively have a BIG impact on achieving the goals of the organization.

But just when organizations need us to Step Up, Step Out, and Be Bold, many of us are being our small selves.

And it is not just that we are keeping ourselves small.

We may wear blinders and not really see other people for who they are. We may make assumptions that put others in a box.

We may block others' ability to be who they are.

We may fear their BIGness.

And, therefore, we may not see others' real potential or capabilities.

||||||||||||||||||||||||||||||||||||||||||||||||||||||||||||||

As a result, many organizations have a culture of smallness, where being small is accepted and expected. Where being small may seem like the safest way to be.

But being small isn't really the safest way for the organization.

Organizations need all their people to be willing to Step Up, Step Out, and Be Bold. To be willing to

  dream BIG

  act BIG

  reach BIG

so that we can

  do our best work TOGETHER.

If this doesn't happen, organizations won't be able to achieve their goals. And soon those organizations will become small—too small to exist.

So we need our organizations to enable all of us to Be BIG.

And each of us as individuals needs to find ways to enable ourselves to **Be BIG**. And each of us needs to support others to **Be BIG**.

And, most importantly, we need to find ways to **Be BIG** *together*.

It will take daring to **Be BIG**.

It will take a willingness to step up and reach for higher goals.

It will take a willingness to step out of our comfort zone and to try new and bold things.

Many of us have learned how to be our small selves. Now we need to learn how to **Be BIG**.

And the payoff will be not just for our organizations but also for ourselves to live fuller lives and reach BIGger dreams. Individually and collectively.

This book is about each of us as individuals being willing to **Be BIG**. It is about our willingness to see others as **BIG**. And it is about finding new ways of partnering so that we can **Be BIG** *together*.

PART ONE

||||||||||||||||||||||||||

ME

Life has taught many of us how to be small by

- not having dreams that are too ambitious.

- not acting too bold.

- not reaching too high.

- not standing out too much!

And yet, many of us want to Be BIG by

- adding value every day.

- expressing who we are.

- engaging ourselves fully.

- stepping up to new challenges.

- stepping out and trying new things.

- being bold and sharing our voice.

Chapter 1 is about the ways we have learned to act small and the messages we tell ourselves that keep us small.

||||||||||||||||||||||
CHAPTER 1

Being my
small self

At times, I may not even be aware that I am being my small self.

At times, I stay small to stay comfortable.

At times, I stay small because I think others will like me better or find me more acceptable.

I make myself small in many ways:

   I do not show up.

   I do not step up.

   I do not speak out.

   I do not share my ideas.

   I do not take up too much space.

Here are some examples of ways I keep myself small.

I stay in my comfort zone

Things are fine the way they are

I have settled into a nice little routine.

I know what is expected from me, and I will deliver just that.

I am seen as competent at what I do, and that's good enough for me.

I can get by with things the way they are. Why should I step out?

Better safe than sorry

I have learned enough to know how to avoid taking risks. Risk taking can be dangerous.

I do things in ways that are familiar to me rather than in new ways.

People often don't notice the things I do right, but they never miss what I do wrong, and they never forget my mistakes. I avoid being noticed.

I know my limitations

This is a large organization, and one person can't make a difference.

Ideas and suggestions are valued only from higher levels in the organization than mine.

I don't know everything and I am sometimes wrong.

I don't want to be a pioneer

Most pioneers died in the wilderness.

Why should I stick my neck out?

I will let someone else volunteer.

Others are not stepping up. Why should I?

I am no hero

Sure, some things aren't fair and some things could be better, but dealing with those things isn't my job.

That is not what I signed up for.

I try not to be seen

I don't let others see me

If I am careful, I can usually get to my work area without anyone seeing me.

I can avoid conversations and confrontations.

I just take notes in meetings. I don't share my thoughts until after the meeting is over, and then only with a few people I really trust.

I don't take up too much space

I stay close to the walls when I am standing in the elevator or walking down the hall.

I just try to stay out of everyone's way.

I keep my head down so I won't be noticed.

I don't stick out

If I look and act like everyone else, I can't be singled out for criticism.

Others can blame all of us, but they can't blame just me.

I don't make waves

I don't ask questions.

I don't complain.

I don't initiate.

I don't report problems.

I don't bring bad news.

I don't rock the boat.

I avoid others

When I pass people in the halls, I don't make eye contact.

If I don't notice others, then maybe they won't notice me.

If I don't want others to bother with me, I stay away from them.

I silence my voice

I keep my thoughts to myself

No one really wants to listen to my ideas.

If others don't hear my ideas, they can't criticize or judge them.

Ideas from people at my level aren't valued anyway.

I spoke up once two years ago and ended up regretting it.

I ration my voice

When it comes to speaking up, it is best to let other people take a turn. That way, I don't get too much notice from the higher-ups or resentment from my colleagues.

If I speak up, others will think I am trying to make them small.

I might not sound smart

I worry what would happen if everyone stopped to listen and I got so nervous that all I could say was, "Umm, er, I ahh, sorry, what I mean is, oh, forget it."

I worry that my ideas might sound dumb.

It has probably been said already anyway

I don't need to say anything; it has all
been said.

I let others represent my point of view.

I don't matter: Why try?

I am a small fish in a BIG pond

What I have to add isn't going to make any difference in the great scheme of things.

No one listens to people at my level (or department or job).

No one really values what I contribute

As long as I do my job and don't make waves, others will leave me alone.

It isn't my job to make suggestions, and that is just fine with me.

I'm not good enough

A lot of people here seem a lot surer of themselves than I am.

It looks like others know something I don't.

I am not sure I fit here

I seem way too different from the people I work with.

I am not sure this is the right place for me.

Few people really listen to my ideas or seem to want me to succeed.

I feel very alone here. Why should I reach out?

This is where it all begins.

||||||||||||||||||||||
CHAPTER 2

Being my BIG self

Chapter 2 is full of ways to Step Up, Step Out, and Be Bold. They are simple, straightforward actions everyone can take.

By doing them, each of us will get BIG.

But there are consequences.

Each of us will take up more space in the world, have more impact, and be more noticeable.

To Be BIG requires each of us to be bold—
to challenge how we have always done things.
To show up in a new way.

To Be BIG, I need to promise myself every day that I will be brave and have the courage to

dream BIG

think BIG

show up BIG

so that I can do my best work.

If I want to Be BIG
I will show up—fully

I am willing to be seen

I have to be willing to give up being invisible and anonymous.

I have to let people see me.

I have to believe I can make a valuable contribution.

I bring my voice, my ideas, my thinking

I am willing to be heard.

I value what I have to say and I expect others will, too.

I am willing to share the parts of me that are different from others, the perspectives that can come only from someone with my unique background and experience—my piece of the puzzle.

I take ownership of my words and deeds

You don't have to agree with me or even think my ideas will work.

I share to provide a different perspective.

And if my idea gives you a different perspective that leads to a better idea, then it was a good contribution, and I am proud of it.

Here I am, warts and all

I don't have to be perfect to be a valuable contributor.

My skills are useful.

My energy is a constantly renewable resource.

I just might bring perspectives that no one else can.

I will tell you what I need

My wants and needs are legitimate.

You are not a mind reader.

I might not be able to get all of what I need or want, but telling you makes it more possible than if I make you guess about it.

I will Step Up
Step Out
Be Bold

I am willing to be myself

Being myself ought to be the most natural thing in the world.

It takes extra energy to be *anything but* myself. I can better use that extra energy to Be BIG.

I am willing to step out of my comfort zones

Comfort can be a sign that I am not reaching high enough.

If I am on comfortable ground, I am not actively engaged in learning and growing.

I am willing to take some risks

I won't take crazy risks or unwarranted risks.

I will take the risks that come with speaking up and being BIG.

I am willing to risk acting awkwardly, being less than perfect, and looking foolish.

I will stand up for what I believe

I give myself permission to decide for myself what my beliefs are.

I will muster up the courage to share with you my deeply held beliefs.

I am willing to forgive myself for not being as BIG today as I will be tomorrow

I am not going to be perfect at being BIG on my first try.

Part of being human is knowing there is no perfect—just doing my best and working to get better.

I am making myself more visible and therefore a larger target for criticism

I will identify and surround myself with people who encourage and support me to Be BIG, but there are bound to be people who don't want me to Be BIG. It comes with the territory.

If I am going to Be BIG, I have to be willing to take the heat.

If things don't work, at least I know I did my part, and I can be proud of me.

I am willing to grow and Be BIG

I am going to dream BIG

I give myself permission to get out of the box that I and others have put me in.

I am challenging myself today to have BIG ideas and BIG thoughts.

I am willing to share those thoughts with others, no matter how wild or dumb people may think they are.

I am going to think BIG

I am challenging myself today to bring my full self with me wherever I go and be my BIG self.

I am not going to make myself small to make others comfortable.

I am going to reach BIG

I am setting my sights high. No one can limit me but me.

I know I am capable of more, and I am striving to reach as far as I can. I know if I do, I can soar.

The better I feel about me, the more able I am to go anywhere and do anything.

I am going to **Be BIG** and do my best work

I am striving for excellence.

I am challenging myself today to set my own bar higher and work to achieve that standard.

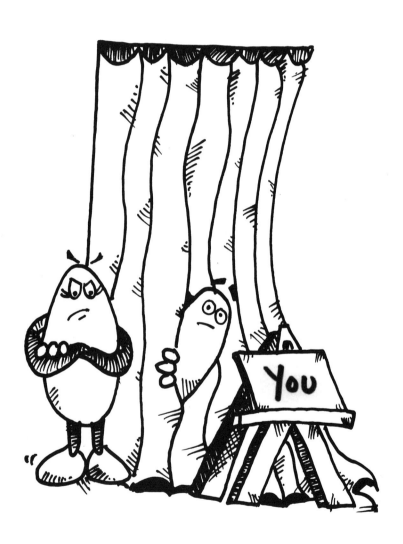

PART TWO

||||||||||||||||||||||||||

YOU

Many of us are aware of how we are diminished by others, by circumstance, by personal history, or by "the system."

Some of us are aware of how we diminish ourselves.

But few of us are aware of the ways in which our behaviors and assumptions may limit and diminish others.

It is not just that others have the potential to Be BIG; they may already exhibit a BIGness that our own smallness cannot see.

I must be daring enough to take my blinders off.

To trust in who YOU are today and who YOU can be tomorrow.

To see the BEST in YOU.

To see the BIG YOU.

Chapter 3 is about the many
ways we intentionally or
unintentionally keep
those around us small.

||||||||||||||||||||||||
CHAPTER 3

Seeing YOU as small

Few of us may want to think we are making others small, and yet we block ourselves from seeing others as their BIG selves.

My assumptions, judgments, and blinders keep me from really seeing the other person who is YOU.

My beliefs and expectations keep YOU in a box that keeps you small.

I don't even realize I am not seeing who YOU are and what is important to YOU.

My blinders block me from understanding what YOU are saying or feeling what YOU are feeling.

What follows are the many ways I keep YOU small and do not see YOU for who you really are or who YOU may become.

I put YOU in a box

I already know what you are like

I am a good judge of character.

I can tell everything I need to know about you by the way you look, the way you dress, and the way you talk.

I already know what you will say and do. I am not going to bother to ask.

I know who you are

Your job title says it all.

People in your role all act the same way.

I know your limitations

I know you are good at a couple of things, but other things are just beyond your role and capabilities.

I know what to expect of you

I am happy when you do your part of the project the way you always do it.

I like you to stick to our established routines.

I feel safest when you stay in your role.

I don't like surprises.

I don't need to get to know you better

This is a workplace, not a social club.

It takes time away from our work to get to know others, and I don't have that time.

I make YOU invisible

I don't pay attention to you

I don't have the energy to give you a lot of attention.

Getting involved with you would take extra effort on my part, and I have enough to do already.

Given your role and mine, I don't think I need to pay attention to you.

I don't really listen to you

I believe I know what you will say even before you say it.

I don't often hear you say things of value.

When you talk, I don't understand you anyway.

We see the world so differently.

When you show up BIG, I believe I am even smaller, so it is best to avoid you.

I don't notice you

I look around the room to see who matters, whose turn it is to speak, or who needs attention, and you don't stand out.

I don't think of you as being on the same team that I am on.

You rarely step up to new challenges, so it is easy to overlook you.

I don't think you can help my future.

I talk right over you

I don't give you space to share your ideas and thoughts.

I don't give you credit for what you do bring up.

I don't allow myself to care about you

I am not going to let you matter to me.

My time is precious, and I have so many important things to do that I don't have space for one more person.

What happens to you doesn't really affect me.

Your problems are your problems.

I don't notice your abilities

I don't see your talents and skills as special

I don't see anything special about what you do or what you can do.

Honestly, anyone can do what you do.

I don't really care how you get the job done as long as it gets done.

I don't think you have anything to add

Your contribution doesn't seem very significant to me.

A lot of people could do it just as well. I probably can do it better.

I don't see how what you have done adds to what we have already created.

I don't learn from what you have done before

I don't know anything about your previous experiences, and anyway, they seem to be irrelevant.

I don't care about your past. What really matters is how you are making a contribution now!

I don't see your potential

I know you keep telling me you can do more, but I just don't see it.

Sometimes it is best to just stick to what you know and not venture out.

I see only your shortcomings

I see and magnify your flaws and sometimes give you that feedback.

You talk about your strengths, but from where I sit, I can only see your weaknesses.

I am just being honest from my point of view.

I don't respect your uniqueness

You are too different from me

You look different and act different, and your ideas are different.

You make me uncomfortable.

I feel like I have to walk on eggshells around you.

Everything seems harder when I am around you.

I don't understand you

I don't understand your ideas and ways of seeing the world.

I don't see the value in your way of thinking.

You have a completely different approach than I do. Since I know my approach works, yours must be wrong.

I don't trust you

People like you make me nervous.

I don't trust your abilities or your motivations.

We hardly ever agree on the best way to do anything.

I once had a bad experience with someone like you.

I don't agree with you

I know my way will work.

My way is the way I have always done things around here.

We don't do things around here like that.

I don't like your style

Your tone of voice, your point of view, and your language grate on me.

The way you walk into a room irritates me.

You need to tone down.

You just don't seem like a good fit.

You are too aggressive, too demanding, too different.

You laugh too loud.

Chapter 4 is about
enabling ourselves to
see our colleagues and
partners as BIG as they
really are. It is about how
we can enable them to
Be BIG and Step Up, Step Out,
and Be Bold to grow.

||||||||||||||||||||||||||
CHAPTER 4

Seeing YOU as BIG

If we support and enable the people around us to Be BIG so that they can do their best work, eventually, we will be surrounded by GIANTS.

And that would be good.

I take my
blinders off

I question my assumptions about you

When it comes down to it, no one ever really fits all my assumptions and generalizations, do they?

I will step out of my box to get to know who you really are.

Not only are you not like others of "your kind," *they are not like you.*

We are all one of a kind.

I won't make you fit into my little box

My expectations are that you will do your best and that you will help me do my best.

I will work to accept and support the many aspects of you.

I will encourage you to let me know if I try to "box" you.

I work to see your point of view

I know I won't always see the world from your perspective, but it is my goal.

When you tell me your ideas, I listen to the context as well as the words. Then I will tell you what I think I heard to make sure I understand what you meant before I respond with my own ideas.

I see you fully

You have thoughts and emotions, a unique background and personal history, and a range of talents and abilities that are different from my own.

You have things you do well and some things you don't do well—and both are always changing.

You have areas in which you are growing and areas that need to be developed.

You are a full in-process being.

I know there is always more

As much as I see you, and as much as I learn about you, I acknowledge that there is always more to be discovered and more that you are becoming.

Seeing you is an ongoing process, not a finite event.

I reach out
and engage

I make it a point to say Hello

When I see you, I make a genuine effort to
connect with you by making eye contact,
shaking hands, saying Hello, or asking about
what is going on in your life (and meaning it)
in ways that are appropriate for the time,
the place, and our relationship.

It takes a little time (though not as much
as I had assumed), but it is worth the effort
to make the connection with you.

I am interested in your life and what is important to you

I like learning from you and hearing what you have to say. It is another view of the world for me—a gift.

I tell you what is going on with me, too

I want you to understand how my mind works and what things are important to me.

I appreciate that you are willing to listen to my stories.

I will support you as I can

Everyone needs support now and then.

I want you to know you can rely on me. If I can help, I will.

I will help you to be your BIG self.

I see your upside

I listen as an ally

When you share your ideas, I assume they have value.

I listen for the nuggets of value, and I will build on and add to your contributions rather than downplay them or find the weaknesses in your ideas.

I see your contributions

You do many things really well and have much to offer.

You really do make a difference, and I will acknowledge that.

Your efforts make a difference, and you set an example for others, too.

I see your potential

Your skills and experience add value,
but what you bring to the table now is
just a moment in time on a path that has
no upper limits.

There is no telling how much more you
could contribute with support and
encouragement.

I support YOU in doing your best work

I support you

My job is to enable you to have a safe place in which you can do your best work.

I am watching your back and making sure that others do, too.

I trust in who you are and in your potential.

I listen to your dreams and help you achieve them

I know you have dreams that are yet unfulfilled. I ask you to share them and to let me know how I can best enable you to achieve them.

I will help you step up and take bold actions to achieve your goals.

I will help you reach for the stars

I will be there for you along the way.

I see all of your potential and perhaps beyond even what you may see for yourself.

I am your cheerleader.

You don't have to Be BIG alone.

PART THREE

||||||||||||||||||||||||||||||||

WE

It is challenging to be a BIG me.
It is even more challenging to see
others as BIG.

But it is most challenging to dare
to Be BIG together.

We keep us small in many ways.

Ways in which we fail to make a
connection, fail to Step Up together,
fail to Step Out into new territory
together, fail to take Bold actions
together.

And yet, if WE are daring enough to
create a new WE, WE can do our best
work together, achieving more than
WE could separately and more than WE
ever dreamed of.

Chapter 5 is about the ways
we avoid working together.
Or, to be more accurate,
working together
successfully. It takes a
positive connection
to create a WE.

||||||||||||||||||||||||
CHAPTER 5
Making ME and YOU small

If I make myself small, I prevent a BIG connection.

If I make you small, I prevent a BIG connection.

But even if I show up fully and even if I really see YOU, plenty of pressures keep us from being BIG together.

Here are some of the attitudes and actions that help ME remain only a ME and prevent us from becoming a WE.

I can do it alone

I don't want anyone meddling in my work

I work long and hard to get things just right, and others want to make changes for no good reason.

Others just want to get their two cents in, to put their own stamp on things.

Why can't others leave well enough alone?

The more people involved, the more time the task will take

It takes so long to make a simple little decision when others are involved: "Let's have a discussion." "Let's get consensus."

Doing it alone would be faster and more efficient.

I don't need you looking over my shoulder

I can do the work without help from others.

I know what I am doing.

I can figure it out on my own.

I don't need others telling me what to do.

A chain is only as strong as its weakest link

I don't want any weak links working with me.

I know with whom I am comfortable.

I don't need the aggravation of breaking in any new team members.

Create a team? I don't know how!

I am not comfortable being a part of a team.

I am afraid of "group think."

I don't want to share the credit.

Things would be a lot easier if others just followed along.

I know what I am doing

I know the task. I know this organization. I know what has worked in the past.

I have gotten by before without the help of others. Why start now?

I protect
my position

I keep things on a need-to-know basis

Knowledge is power. The information I have about the organization's strategies and decisions and my job won't give me an edge if I just give it away to others.

I will dole out information only as necessary or in return for a little quid pro quo.

Why should I help others?

What have others ever done for me?

If I help others succeed, it takes away from my success.

If someone else drags me down, then we both fail. Nobody ever helped me.

Helping others allows weak people to succeed. Going it alone is how I succeed.

I don't like to share personal information

I don't want to give other people too much power.

I am not sure I feel safe enough to share information about me with other people.

If I tell others something, they might use it against me.

I won't waste my energy to help others

It is hard enough getting the resources that I need. I can't help others. Besides, we are all competing for the same resources.

The better others look, the worse off I will be.

I believe in the chain of command

If I don't report to you, I don't have to listen to you.

And if you report to me, please don't speak until you are spoken to.

If you are from another group, or if you are at the same level as I am, you can't give me orders, and I don't want your opinions.

Clear and strict roles are predictable and easy to deal with.

I don't trust others

The more control I keep, the more comfortable I feel

I don't like too many moving parts in the machinery.

If I handle things, I will know where everything is and when something is going to happen. There won't be any conflict or confusion.

If I am in control, others will have to come to me for information or with requests.

I don't have time to try other people's way

Maybe if we weren't under constant time pressures, I could let some new people have a turn, but this is no time for experiments.

Anyway, it takes too long to get others up to speed.

It is too risky

If I try other people's way of doing things, there is no telling how it could turn out.

What is in it for me?

If I try this "we" thing and it fails, I will look bad. If I try it and it works, others will look good and get the credit.

I don't want to share credit with other people. It could limit my opportunities.

Really working as a team is impossible

Whenever I try to put a team together, I can't trust that others will pull their weight.

If I get a loser on the team, I will lose.

I don't reach out

I don't want to make the first move

It is no fun being rejected. I would look foolish.

I am shy and don't feel comfortable making the first move.

I would prefer to keep my distance

I don't want to be best friends with the people I work with.

I come here to do a job and get paid.

I don't want to hear others' troubles or their life histories.

I have my own life and my own friends outside these walls.

I don't want to let down my guard

I am not going to talk about my concerns.

I don't want others to see my weaknesses.

I don't want to have a whole team relying on me and judging me.

I have always worked alone

I know how to be successful working
by myself.

I don't want to work with others.

I am afraid I won't be as successful working
with others.

I don't need anyone else

I have always been told it is a weakness to
need others.

I am not sure I even know how to ask for
help from others.

Chapter 6 is about ways
we can combine our thinking,
skills, and energies to build
greater things than we
ever could apart.

|||||||||||||||||||||||||
CHAPTER 6

ME and YOU BIG together

We are entering unfamiliar territory.

It just might be

(UH OH!)

the land of WE—where everyone has the potential to become a GIANT.

And we would be among them. It is a land of empowering partnerships we can reach only when we recognize that we need each other to do our best and be our best—to Be BIG together.

Here is what we can do to get there.

WE need others

We need each others' competencies

I am not going to continue to pretend I am the best at everything. Too many skills are needed.

I can't do everything.

I need other people whose competencies, experiences, and perspectives complement my own.

We all need to be in the game

If we are going to succeed over the long haul, everybody needs to be willing to Step Up and Step Out together, to Be BIG and get smarter as we go.

We will last longer if we are all in the game and we don't let any one person carry too much of the load.

We need more sets of eyes

I can see in only one direction at a time.

I can only see out of my own set of lenses.

To get a full, high-definition, 360-degree view of things, I need to partner with others who look in different directions and see things differently than I do.

We get better ideas together

The people who are most different from me often come up with ideas I would never imagine. Those ideas give me new ideas.

My new ideas give you even newer ideas.

Pretty soon, we are in a Land of GIANTS, a land none of us could ever get to individually.

WE are open and willing to engage

We are willing to trust each other

We give each other the benefit of the doubt.

We know we will get better as we work together.

We behave as if we are already proven partners.

We accept and understand each other's point of view

Each of us has a way of looking at things that can help all of us learn and grow.

We constantly seek new partners

We have a need for fresh eyes to enable us to grow.

We need new partners to add value to our team.

Each new point of view and set of skills adds to our capabilities, our potential and our completeness, collectively and individually.

We are on a journey of discovery

Getting in sync with new partners and a team is a learning process that means growth for all.

We make a commitment to learn more about each other's talents and what we each need to do our best work together.

We are willing to really listen and learn from each other.

WE ALL need to grow

Your growth does not limit my ability to grow

This is not a zero-sum game: there is plenty of room for all of us to grow.

If you get BIG, it doesn't make any of us smaller.

In fact, the BIGger you get, the easier it will be for each one of us to Be BIG.

We watch each other's back

We will let each other know when we think we are not being our best or not being the person we want to be.

We will provide support so that each of us has a safe space to continue to learn and grow.

We will hang in there

We will partner through the tough times as well as the good times. Getting through tough times together is what partnership and learning are all about.

We won't always agree

If we agree on everything, we will never learn anything new from each other.

The best part of partnering is bringing different ideas to the partnership. If we brought only the same things, we would be redundant!

This is a learning experience for us, and we can learn and grow through our differences and disagreements.

In fact, if we are not disagreeing, we may not be bringing our full selves to our work.

We are committed to learning about how to make this WE thing work.

We each may have doubts that this WE thing is going to work, but I will do my part and I will help you do yours.

It cannot be one way.

It all comes down to a commitment to create a BIG WE.

We will show up to partner

We will give ourselves time to build a WE

We commit to building the partnership and that means being willing to invest in learning about each other.

A WE won't happen just because we say we are partners.

We are willing to put in the time and effort required to create the WE that we want to be.

We will each work at bringing our full selves

We each take responsibility for bringing our full selves to the team, not just to do our part of the work, but to continually develop ourselves to become better partners.

We will create a safe place for our ideas to come out to play and join in our partnership.

We will take our blinders off and see each other for who we are

We all make assumptions.

We are filled with stereotypes built into us by our cultures.

We each need to be willing to own and recognize our blinders when they appear and then let them go, move on, and create something BIG together.

We will strive to do our best TOGETHER

We will dream BIG dreams together

Each of us has dreams and we are willing to create a collective dream that is BIG—BIGger than any one of ours individually.

We will act together as a WE

We will bring our ideas, excitement, energy, and passion to our WE.

We will learn from our WE, share differences of perspective and opinion, and have conflicts and intense engagement.

When we make a decision, we will act as one and stand behind the decision we have made as a WE.

We will challenge ourselves to grow

We will set goals that stretch us and take on projects that challenge us to Be BIG.

We know our combined wisdom and talent will help us reach beyond our individual capabilities.

We will define success based on our collective efforts

When we really get our partnership engine cranking, there is no telling where it will take us.

We will focus on what it takes to achieve our goals and not worry about whether the destination is too far, too high, or too BIG.

We are committed to doing our best work together, and will do what it takes to achieve success.

We know that when WE succeed based on our collective energy and work, we all succeed.

‖‖‖

Conclusion
daring to do our best work TOGETHER

If I bring my full self and Step Up, Step Out, and Be Bold

If I take off my blinders and really see you

And if you do the same
TOGETHER, WE can do our best work.

And Be BIG—

BIGger than anyone could imagine.

It starts with me—daring to believe I matter. Getting out of my comfort zone and having the courage to step up, step out, and stand tall. Being willing to show up fully, giving my best, being my BIG self, so that **I can do my best work**.

But that is not enough.

I then must be daring enough to see YOU. I must take my blinders off to reach out and engage YOU and support YOU in your journey as an individual so that YOU can be your best BIG self **and do YOUR best work**.

But that is still not enough.

Because this just creates the possibility of a WE.

ME and YOU need to be daring enough to see each other as BIG and to partner in ways **to do OUR best work together**.

So how do we start?

Step Up:

To the challenge of being BIG.

To new responsibilities.

To the opportunities for growth and partnership.

Step Out:

Of old routines.

From your small self and seeing others as small.

Into the light, where you can be seen and see others.

Be Bold:

By speaking up rather than remaining silent.

By identifying places where it is safe to be your BIG self. Or making places safe enough to risk being BIG.

By finding others who are being their BIG selves from whom to learn and grow.

DARE to:

Stand up for yourself.

Consider new ideas.

Make mistakes.

Encourage others to contribute.

Create new thoughts,

new dreams,

new possibilities.

The challenge is yours.

Are you willing to be bold enough, daring enough as an individual and with others

so that you can **live among GIANTS**?

Because if you do, "I promise you a richer and more exciting life"—for you and for us all.

|||||||||||||||||||||||||||||||||||||||||||||||||||||||||

Acknowledgments

Our writing and thinking partners: Mickey Bradley, Roger Gans, and Tara Whittle. Special thanks to each of you for bringing your uniqueness and talents to make this book a reality.

Ilene Kane, thank you for your shepherding of this book.

Our publisher, especially Steven Piersanti, who always with love pushes us to reach inside and think BIG, dream BIG, and act BIG. Thanks, Steve. You enable us to do our best work.

Our illustrator, Jeevan Sivasubramaniam, thank you for your patience and your creativity. Your spirit has been inspirational to us from the first time we met.

Kamen Miller, thank you for your lettering.

Thanks to Dianne Platner, Michael Crowley, Richard Wilson, Jeremy Sullivan, and the rest of the BK staff for your hard work and commitment to *Be BIG*.

Our readers/reviewers: thank you, Douglas Hammer, Perviz Randeria, and Regina Sacha for being our thinking partners in this project. Each of your insights helped make this book stronger and BIGger.

David B. Levine and Pauline Kamen Miller, thank you for being our wonderful and supportive marriage partners and enabling us to go out in the world so we can Be BIG. And Zak and Willow, our dogs, who treat us like we are BIG every day.

The leaders and Core Inclusion Partners at Allstate Technology and Operations, with a special thanks to John Bader, who models how to Be BIG with every interaction.

All the friends, colleagues, and clients who have helped us be our BIG selves and who have been their BIG selves so we could do our best work together.

Those who gave us your thinking along the way and therefore influenced our thinking and writing, including Yvonne Alverio, Cheeneah Armstrong, Monica Biggs, Marilyn Blair, Carol Brantley, Arthur Brown, L. David Brown, Kathy Clements, Jane Covey, Dennis DaRos, Valerie Davis-Howard, Keith Earley, Denny Gallagher, Pat Gardner, Lewis Gasorek, Bill Gathen, John Gavares, Jim Gundell, Sarah Halley, Effenus Henderson, Bailey Jackson, Corey L. Jamison, Masonna Johnson, Paula Jones, Deb Kendall, Rick Kremer, Holly Krohel, Daniel Levine, Marian Mankin, K. McArthur, Karon Moore, Peter Norlin, Coleen Paratore, Angela Park, Charles Pfeffer, Debbie Plager, Monica Poindexter, Maria Racho, Jae Requiro, Andy Satter, Nan Satter, Susan Schor, Charlie Seashore, Kristin Sheridan, Molly Singer, Paul Singer, Cindy Szadokierski, Randy Tosch,

Elizabeth Vales, John Vegas, Catherine Volk, Craig Washington, Mary Frances Winters, and Elizabeth Young.

And the Lake House, for being a beautiful restful "thinking" place in which we can think BIG thoughts.

|||||||||||||||||||||||||||||||||||||||||||||||||||||||

About the Authors

Judith H. Katz

Fueled by her passion for addressing systemic barriers and known for her boundless energy and sharp analytical mind, Judith H. Katz brings more than thirty years of experience to her work in strategic culture change. Her work is an extension of her lifelong commitment to championing respect for all people and social justice, and she was recently recognized for this by *Profiles in Diversity Journal*, which named her one of forty Pioneers of Diversity. As Executive Vice President of The Kaleel Jamison Consulting Group, Inc., Dr. Katz assists organizations to create sustainable and highly successful inclusion change efforts that, when integrated with business strategies, can achieve enhanced bottom-line results. She has consulted with many organizations, including Allstate, Dun & Bradstreet; E. I. du Pont de Nemours and Company; Eileen Fisher, Inc.; Singapore Telecommunications Ltd.; Toyota Motor Sales; and United Airlines. A former academic, Judith is a dynamic speaker and internationally known author. The twenty-fifth anniversary of her landmark book, *White Awareness: Handbook for Anti-Racism Training* (University of Oklahoma Press, 1978, 2003), has been celebrated with the publication of a revised edition. Her courageous autobiographical work, *No Fairy Godmothers, No Magic Wands: The Healing Process After Rape* (RBE Publishers, 1984), was one of the first of its kind to assist rape survivors in the recovery process. She is coeditor of *The Promise of Diversity* (McGraw-Hill, 1994) and coauthor, with Frederick A. Miller, of *The Inclusion Breakthrough: Unleashing the Real Power of Diversity* (Berrett-Koehler, 2002). Judith is the recipient of the 2003 Diversity Training University International Cultural Competency Professional Award and the 2004 American College Personnel Association Voice of Inclusion Medallion.

Frederick A. Miller
Frederick A. Miller is the CEO and Lead Client Strategist of The Kaleel Jamison Consulting Group, Inc. A pioneer and leading authority on creating cultures of inclusion that are high performing, he was noted in *The Age of Heretics* (Currency Doubleday, 1996) as one of the forerunners of corporate change and was named by *Profiles in Diversity Journal* as one of forty Pioneers of Diversity. In his thirty-plus years of experience, he has worked with many senior-level executives from such renowned companies as Mobil, Dupont, Toyota, Foxwoods Casino, Eileen Fisher, Inc., Wild Planet Toys, Northeast Utilities, United Airlines, and Apple Computers. Fred has been

involved with many founders as they transition from a "foundercentric" culture to one of a professional management staff. Fred was involved with this transition at Ben & Jerry's Homemade Holdings, Inc., where he was on the board of directors for eight years. He also is the founder of the Institute for Inclusion, a nonprofit organization that provides a forum for the exploration, definition, and distribution of the principles, values, and best practices of Inclusion in the workplace and in communities. Fred is respected for his ability to examine a system, issue, or organizational culture at multiple levels and quickly translate his observations into a customized, strategic vision and change-oriented action. He is coauthor, with Judith H. Katz, of *The Inclusion Breakthrough: Unleashing the Real Power of Diversity* (Berrett-Koehler, 2002), and managing editor of *The Promise of Diversity* (McGraw-Hill, 1994). Fred received the Outstanding Service Award from the Organization Development Network (OD Network) in 2000, the Lifetime Achievement Award from the OD Network in 2007, and the Asia-Pacific HRM Congress HR Leadership Award in 2008.

Berrett–Koehler
Publishers

A community dedicated to creating
a world that works for all

Visit Our Website: www.bkconnection.com

Read book excerpts, see author videos and Internet movies, read
our authors' blogs, join discussion groups, download book apps,
find out about the BK Affiliate Network, browse subject-area
libraries of books, get special discounts, and more!

Subscribe to Our Free E-Newsletter, the *BK Communiqué*

Be the first to hear about new publications, special discount
offers, exclusive articles, news about bestsellers, and more! Get
on the list for our free e-newsletter by going to **www
.bkconnection.com**.

Get Quantity Discounts

Berrett-Koehler books are available at quantity discounts for
orders of ten or more copies. Please call us toll-free at (800)
929-2929 or email us at **bkp.orders@aidcvt.com**.

Join the BK Community

BKcommunity.com is a virtual meeting place where people
from around the world can engage with kindred spirits to create
a world that works for all. **BKcommunity.com** members may
create their own profiles, blog, start and participate in forums
and discussion groups, post photos and videos, answer surveys,
announce and register for upcoming events, and chat with others
online in real time. Please join the conversation!

SUSTAINABLE FORESTRY INITIATIVE
Label applies to the text stock

Certified Fiber
Sourcing
www.sfiprogram.org